SO WHAT'S THE POINT?

If You Have Ever Asked

Holly Fourchalk, PhD., DNM®, RHT, HT

CHOICES UNLIMITED
FOR
HEALTH AND WELLNESS

Copyright 2014 © Choices Unlimited for Health and Wellness

Dr. Holly Fourchalk, Ph.D., DNM®, RHT, HT

Tel: 604.764.5203
Fax: 604.465.7964

Website: www.choicesunlimited.ca
E-mail: holly@choicesunlimited.ca

Editing, Interior Design and Cover Design:
Wendy Dewar Hughes, Summer Bay Press

ISBN: 978-1-927626-40-5
Digital ISBN: 978-1-927626-41-2

DISCLAIMER

Every effort has been made by the author to ensure that the information in this book is as accurate as possible. However, it is by no means a complete or exhaustive examination of all information.

The author knows what worked for her and what has worked for others but no two people are the same. Therefore, the author cannot and does not render judgment or advice regarding a particular individual.

Further, because each person is unique, any two individuals may experience different results from the same therapy.

The author believes in both prevention and the superiority of a natural non-invasive approach over drugs and surgery.

The information collected within comes from a variety of researchers and sources from around the world. This information has been accumulated in the western healing arts over the past thirty years.

It is not the intent of the author that anyone should choose to read this book and make decisions regarding his or her personal beliefs based on ideas contained in this book.

The author and publisher are not responsible for any adverse effects or consequences resulting from the use of any of the suggestions or information contained in the book but offer this material as information that the public has a right to hear and utilize at its own discretion.

To my Parents

For all their support and encouragement
My Dad for his ever-listening ear
My mother for her open mind

CONTENTS

Introduction
CHAPTER 1 7
Why do we ask the question?
CHAPTER 2 13
Religions from East to West—So what's the point?
CHAPTER 3 21
From East to West Psychologically—So what's the point?
CHAPTER 4 32
What about people who are not criminals but cause chaos for everyone else?
CHAPTER 5 36
Actions and Consequences
CHAPTER 6 46
Relationships—is there a point?
CHAPTER 7 64
What is the point of suffering?
CHAPTER 8 68
Why do we compare?
CHAPTER 9 77
What about when we try hard without achieving what we are struggling for in business?
CHAPTER 10 88
What about when we are struggling for weight issues without apparent success?
CHAPTER 11 96
What about when we are struggling for our health without apparent success
CHAPTER 12 105
Does time contribute to what's the point?
CHAPTER 13 113
What purpose does the question served in our lives?
CHAPTER 14 119
Conclusion

INTRODUCTION

Have you ever asked yourself—what's the point? Most people have at some time in their lives, if not regularly throughout life. Many ask the question as they are going through difficult ordeals. Others ask themselves when they have gone through the ordeal. Some ask at critical points in their life, such as during a mid-life crisis. Some need to have a purpose or reason for being. Some ask out of sheer curiosity. The question can take on various forms:

> What's the point to life?
> What's the purpose of being here?
> Why bother working a lifetime?
> What's the point of my job?
> What's the point of going through all the "hell" in life?
> What's the point of going through all the challenges in life?

Some take a somewhat different approach and ask: Is this all there is?

So why do we ask the question? We tend to ask the question "what is the point?" for some basic reasons. The first concerns finding meaning as a species in the cosmos. The second is to find one's specific purpose in our own individual life. The third is when actions, whether negative or positive, our own or the actions of others, don't appear to have the consequence we expect them to have. The fourth is to find meaning in our suffering. All reasons that provoke questioning stem from a quest for meaning.

Ultimately, it is a very good question to ask, regardless of the spin you put on it. The more challenging element, however, is how you answer yourself. If you come up with an answer that gives your life meaning and purpose, you have hit the jackpot. Or at least for as long as that answer suffices. However, if you learn what you need to learn at that particular stage of life, and you move onto the next stage of life, you may find yourself asking the question asking—perhaps from a different perspective.

When you are in a place in your life where you have found a great answer to your question, good for you. That is a great place to be—although most people tend to "waste" it.

How do you waste a time like that in your life? Well, many will see it as a waste if you choose not to embrace growth, learning and increased awareness. For many Westerners, if not for all peoples around the world, we get lazy when:

- Life feels good
- Our needs are met
- We have a sense of purpose

We settle. We get comfortable. We enjoy the time with complacency. We don't push to continue to grow, learn, and

So What's the Point?

develop our awareness. In effect, we get lazy.

Ultimately, I think this time, when life is so giving and feels so good, is the best time to push boundaries, to dig deeper, to ask further. But that takes determination, discipline, self-initiative, and awareness that many don't have. If, however, we choose to push during these good times, I believe it makes the more difficult times easier to move through. In fact, we may not require the more difficult times to push us to develop our understanding and awareness and reach our greater potential.

People who do this are the dedicated explorers, who will take even this time in life to push their boundaries, to reach for their greater potential, and explore their abilities, talents, and inner selves. We will explore these kinds of people later on in the book.

If, however, you provided yourself with an answer that does not provide meaning to your life then you are in trouble. That trouble may lead into depression and/or despair, anxiety, avoidance, repression, addictions (a method of self-medicating until you find an answer that work for you—although the probability of that greatly diminishes when you get caught up in addictions). We will also explore depression and addictions further later in this book.

Am I going to give you the ultimate answer in this book? No! What I do hope to provide you with is some concepts, philosophies, and methods of finding an answer that does work for you at whatever stage you are in life. There may never be the right answer, the only answer. But there is *your* answer. Furthermore, as you grow and develop in awareness of your life, you will find that your answers change. That is a good sign. It means you are evolving and not stuck.

Whether you believe in God, or Source/Universal Oneness/Evolution, you might say, "You were given a brain so now is the time to use it". While that is true, we need to go way beyond the brain's capacity to function.

The whole idea of figuring out what the point is is that the answer is very unique and specific to each person. There are different ways of finding a good answer for you so we will need to cover a lot of territory and a lot of possibilities.

Use this book well. Make lots of notes. Use highlighters if you like. Make the book your study. If you do this, you will find the method that resonates the most with you right now. You may need to read the book again, at another point in your life, in order to determine a different method that will resonate with you then *or* you may find that the same method works for you repeatedly. Again, there are no absolutes—only choices.

By the way, the name of my company is Choices Unlimited for Health and Wellness because there is an infinite number of choices or ways to be out of balance *and* an infinite number of choices/way/modalities to get back into balance. Even within a given modality there are numerous different methods. For example, psychology has behavioral, cognitive, cognitive-behavioral, humanistic, interpersonal, and psychodynamic techniques. Whenever anyone claims that one way is the be all and end all, you might want to look elsewhere. There is a huge number of choices and that is one of your main tenants of being human—you were given free choice. Find the choice that resonates most with you and allow yourself to move through it onto the next.

If you keep an open mind, allow your mind to expand, develop your awareness, go through the exercises and allow yourself to explore your inner self then the book will have achieved what I set out to achieve.

For some people, reading this book may be the first exploration of self, purpose, and meaning of life that they have ever attempted. For others, this will be "old hat" and hopefully provide the necessary tools to move on to the next steps of their journeys. Wherever you are starting from, I wish you all the best in your journey. Just remember that the journey never ends. It is about the journey, not the destination. This is not about "getting there". This is about how to work the journey to the best of your capacity; how to get the subconscious to do a lot of the work for you and how to embrace and enjoy the journey along the way.

You can choose to be like my mother, who reads the first chapter and then the last to determine if she wants to read the book but if you choose that route you will have missed the essence of the book. But life is all about choices. You get to choose.

I hope that you will choose to:

- Explore the journey
- Laugh at yourself
- Work through some challenges
- Let go of some old beliefs and attitudes
- Have fun
- Read and study with an open mind
- Develop your awareness
- Choose to enjoy your journey

CHAPTER 1
Why do we ask the question?

Why do we ask the question, if the question can cause so much pain and suffering? If the answer may only work for us in the short term or if the answer is really subjective without an absolute answer, why do we bother to ask the question?

Well, we could answer this question simply and just say: because it is a good question. But there is far more to it than that.

As we already said, it is a question that most people have asked at some point in their lives. It is a natural response question to a huge number of life situations. Let's first look at when and why we generally ask the question, so what is the point?

Philosopher Reasons

Whether we look to current philosophers or go back to historical philosophers, i.e. Aristotle, Socrates, Plato, or the philosophers amongst our friends and family, we find that they continue to search and explore:

- Why we as a species are here in the universe?
- Where did we come from?
- Are we the only intelligent beings in the universe?

- What is the point in being here?
- Where did we come from?
- What is our purpose?
- What is the point?

Any individual may philosophically explore these questions in response to their own existence. Philosophers tend to ask the question from a more generic place—why are we all here? What is the point to humanity? Within that larger context, they may also be asking or looking for purpose to their own existence. But the more generic philosophical question applies to why we are all here.

When philosophy looks at the individual question, it tends to be at a far deeper level and how that deeper level connects with the bigger picture. They don't tend to look at why an individual may get away with poor choices or poor behaviors or a lack of responsibilities. They look more from a global point of view: Why are we *all* here? Many answers have evolved over the centuries.

Ayurvedic philosophy tends to be recognized as the oldest philosophy known on earth. In very simple terms, they see the universe as originating simply from "awareness". From "awareness" came "intent", the original yin and yang, if you wish.

Awareness and intent combined and thus we have the many stages of creation.

Religious/Spiritual Reasons

Whether we define ourselves as religious, or spiritual, or atheist, a natural question is why we are here, and what is the point? We look for purpose in life. We want our lives to be meaningful. We want our lives to have value. If we can't give reason or purpose to our lives we circle back to that question.

Christianity

Christianity tells us that God has a purpose for our lives. We need to believe in God, dedicate our lives to Christ, and our purpose will unfold. Unfortunately, there are many who have believed that they have accepted Christ as their savior, seem to dedicate their lives to serving the Lord, and may still question. So that alone does not always answer the question.

Catholicism tells us that our efforts to live this kind of "Christ-like" life will assure us our place in heaven. Protestantism tells us that grace was already brought down to us through Christ but that our responsibility is to live a Christ-filled life. Both look to God and to Christ to give us a purpose in life and to attempt to answer the question—what is the point?

Buddhism

Buddhism tells us that the point of life is the accumulation and/or disbursement of karma. The extent to which we accumulate positive or negative karma in this life will impact our sojourn through another life. Now, some see the karmic process as a punishment or reward system, while others see it as an opportunity for growth, learning, and awareness. Ultimately, karma simply means actions have consequences.

Most agree that the karmic process is a journey of developing our capacity for compassion and balance through all aspects of our lives.

The statement "every action or choice has a consequence" doesn't just apply to negatives but also to positives. In addition, we are not guaranteed of a particular consequence. Choices made from the highest morals or with the best intentions also have consequences and while they tend to have a better probability of good consequences, it is not guaranteed. No matter what choice we make or from what level of responsibility or morality we come, there will be consequences. Everything has consequences.

Sometimes it will appear that those behaviors or choices that come from the highest levels of morality or intentions have negative consequences, such as when you thought you were being honorable, or responsible, or doing your due diligence and you still feel like you got the short end of the stick.

You might have had a situation in your life whereby you came from an honorable, moral perspective and did your due diligence when wham! Something went totally sideways and you suffered. And you ask, so what was the point?

You might have made a legal agreement, got into a relationship, been careful and conscientious but something went sideways and you lost out.

One might look at the Dalai Lama, acknowledged as a very highly developed human being in Buddhist philosophy, yet look at what he has suffered in his lifetime.

New Age

New Age beliefs often take a somewhat different perspective from the others mentioned. While historically, the religious framework presented held that responsibility was the cornerstone of morality and spirituality, responsibility is often overlooked today in western societies under the guise of New Age spirituality. Actually, New Age beliefs are not new at all. They are combinations of old Eastern religious beliefs brought to the west.

What makes these philosophies "new" is that historically the gurus held them, considered the upper echelons of spiritual development. They were not known to the Western societies and especially not to the masses in Western societies.

When these Eastern beliefs were brought to masses in Western culture through individuals like Yogananda (author of Autobiography of a Yogi) and the Maharishi, they were misunderstood and abused. They did, however, resurrect that old philosophical question, what is the point?

Stop and ask yourself:

- Are you asking the question – so what is the point?
- If you are asking the question – why are you asking the question?
- If you are not asking the question – why are you not asking the question?
- Off the top of your head, what is your current answer to the question?

CHAPTER 2

Religions from the East to the West—
So what's the point?

Western philosophies and Eastern philosophies tend to have a basic difference. Eastern philosophies are less likely to be polarized in their tenets. What does this mean? Polarized thinking works in terms of opposites, such as, us and them, black and white, good and evil, love and hate, etc.

In psychology, this style of thinking tends to be considered immature but we will save subject that for another chapter.

Western religions, more so than other philosophies, tend to be more about us and them. For instance, the concept of if you are not with us you are against us tends to be the basis of Christianity. Thus, some Christians believed they had to go out and conquer the world and hopefully convert everyone to Christianity.

Now, a Christian might argue that the reason for conversion is so that no one would go to hell at the time of death. However, not everyone believes there is a hell. Many believe that there are various planes of existence or that each plane has a continuum.

This philosophy supports the concept that on the next plane, heaven and hell are just at different ends of the continuum. Christians do not hold with this view.

In fact, Christianity is known for going throughout the world and attempting to "convert" people to belief in Christ. And, like other religions elsewhere, cultures, languages, and other philosophies are changed in the process.

In contract to this black and white style of thinking, Buddhists would never attempt to convert you to Buddhism. Rather than attempt to convert you to their philosophy of life, they would rather support you in actualizing or optimizing whatever religion you already belong to. In Buddhism, everyone is part of the process.

In addition to exclusion versus inclusion, there is another major difference between Eastern and Western thinking, that is, responsibility.

Often Eastern philosophies lose the impact of their deeper meanings and important subtleties in the translation from the Eastern masters to the Western masses. For instance, an important and obvious (versus subtle) concept that was lost to many in the translation was responsibility. Let's look at this concept as it has huge implications in understanding what the point is.

So What's the Point?

Many, unfortunately, have taken responsibility out of the tenant of "learning to live in the moment". Living in the moment and appreciating the moment to its full is extremely important. This doesn't mean eliminating the past and the future. There is responsibility in recognizing and utilizing both the past and the future well.

For many, especially in Eastern beliefs, such as Buddhism, Zen, Hinduism etc., developing responsibility is the basis for developing morality, and morality is the basis for developing spirituality. In fact, in old India of long ago the class system was based on this. You were not born into a given class. The class you belonged to was determined by your behavior.

- Lowest class had no sense of responsibility.
- Next class included those who recognized that their behavior had consequences and took responsibility.
- Next class not only had a sense of responsibility but were learning higher levels of morality.
- The highest class not only had a developed sense of responsibility and a developed sense of morality but were now developing spiritually.

So let's take a closer look at this.

From a Western Judaic perspective, spirituality comes from a very different place. From a Christian perspective, for instance, we have two belief systems:

- Catholicism teaches that we have to earn our grace and therefore we must preform our deeds, such as, say our prayers and our "Mother Marys".

- Protestants believe that grace was brought down to us in the form of Jesus and therefore all we need to do is "commit to the Lord".

In older times there was much greater emphasis put on living a spiritual life but today either can be more about religion than spirituality, though this is not always the case.

Let's go back to more Eastern beliefs for a moment. To develop spirituality we need to recognize that actions have consequences, and as such, we are thus responsible for each decision we make. Whether we choose to be responsible or not; whether we want to be responsible or not, it doesn't matter. The fact that your choices influence your future is as stable and consistent as gravity. You can deny gravity or you can try to pretend it's not there but ultimately it doesn't change anything. The laws of gravity continue whether we want them to or not. Gravity simply is. Sure, we can build airplanes to fly and we can even blast out of our atmosphere and go to the moon but look at how we had to orchestrate around gravity to do that. Gravity didn't change.

The same occurs with responsibility. We can pretend it doesn't have an effect and we can try to ignore it or pretend that we are above it or that it doesn't apply to us. It remains.

There is a subtle difference between blaming someone for your actions and recognizing what impact that person had on your choices. For instance, recognizing that you are responsible for a given action while also recognizing what someone taught you is owning the impact another's viewpoint had on your decision. Blame would simply be to blame them and hold them accountable for your actions. People without a developed sense of moral function have a difficult time seeing the difference.

Many are unaware of their responsibility for their choices and simply blame others out of habit. Many others don't want to take responsibility for their actions because it may mean:

- They are a bad person.
- They may have to pay for their actions.
- They will have to re-evaluate their whole life.
- They may not continue as they are used to doing.
- The guilt they would have to bear would be too great.
- It would alter their sense of control in the situation.

For a psychopath, it may simply mean he couldn't care less. According to Western Psychology, psychopaths see other people as simply objects to be used to meet his gratification and he has no sense of morals or compassion, sympathy or empathy for others.

Many may argue that many criminals get away with crimes they have committed. Abusive parents and partners can often get away with their crimes. Sociopaths live around the world and in all levels of society and often die without any apparent reckoning for their activities. Sociopaths do well in war torn countries but also abound in non-war countries. And all these arguments are true. Society isn't always capable of "punishing" crimes. In the justice system, as with many other systems, many don't get their "just rewards" as society would have it. Victims are often further victimized while criminals appear to get off without punishment. And when this happens, people will ask, "So what's the point?"

That doesn't mean that committing the crime doesn't have an effect. Learning to avoid or deny or rationalize our choices still has consequences. For most of us, it affects us mentally, emotionally, spiritually, as well as the world around us.

What does it mean to be responsible? There are different perspectives, as noted above, and they differentiate what you should be responsible for. Let's go over a few of them.

So What's the Point?

1. Responsible for your actions – that one is pretty basic.
2. Responsible for your thoughts. Do you have command over your thoughts or do they have command over you?
3. Do you know what your underlying life themes are and are they in control of you or are you in control of them?
4. Do you know what your value system is and how it influences your choices?
5. Have you identified the automatic assumptions you have made about life and determined whether they were modeled to you, or taught to you? Did you choose them in reaction to your parents or did you decide upon them?
6. Responsibility for your emotions. Do you control your emotions, or do they control you? This is what emotional intelligence is all about.
7. Responsible for your belief system – what you believe about life, the afterlife, God, or Universal oneness; about evolution and about this plain of existence?
8. Responsible for your definitions in life. For instance, what are your definitions of the following:
    - Love
    - Forgiveness

- Awareness
- Appreciation
- Acceptance
- Boundaries
- Spirituality vs. religion

EXERCISE:

If you belonged to an ancient Indian society, what social class do you think you would belong to and why?

Take each of the above responsibility issues, and identify how responsible you think you are for each?

Define each of the words in #8.

CHAPTER 3

From East to West Psychologically—
So what's the point?

Western psychology also looks at this process but from a different perspective. One important contributor to understanding how the mind works was Dr. Beck. In the process of studying how people defended their egos, protected their perception of reality and justified how they functioned, Beck came up with a list of what are now called Becks Cognitive Distortions. (Note: since that time, many others have come up with various lists as well.) These cognitive distortions recognize different ways that we can distort information and include:

"All or none" thinking

This means thinking in absolutes, such as, it has to be this way or that way, rather than looking for alternative solutions. "I want it all or nothing" as opposed to looking for something that benefits all. People who think this way will turn away from opportunities because they cannot get all that they want.

Black and white thinking is very similar to all or none. In black and white thinking, people use words like "always" and "never", as opposed to "sometimes", "usually", or "often".

Unfortunately, these people tend to write off an entire event, person, or concept when they see a single flaw. Admiration can easily turn into contempt in cases like this.

Emotional reasoning

Emotional reasoning is a fairly common approach. It was recognized and explored in the text of the book, *Emotional Intelligence,* by Daniel Goleman, and is now a common term that is even used in cartoons.

Emotional reasoning refers to making a cognitive determination based to your feelings rather than the evidence at hand. An example of this would be someone who favours a given political party because of how he feels rather than because of the candidate's political platforms, or the character of the representative.

Jumping to conclusions

Jumping to conclusions is another form of cognitive distortion. There are two major types of recognized patterns:

- Inference, which is assuming that you know or understand another person's thoughts based on their behavior or nonverbal communications, all without asking them.

- Fortune telling is the other way of jumping to conclusions. Usually this is a negative prediction—the expectation that something will turn out negative—without sufficient evidence or without acknowledging the evidence to the contrary.

Labeling/Mislabeling

Labeling could be identified as an extreme type of overgeneralization. When we assume that a particular behavior is indicative of the whole person rather than an isolated incident that may provide an entirely different understanding.

Magnification and Minimization

Both of these are cognitive distortions and so common that we even have sayings for them: "Don't make a mountain out of a molehill," and "Don't sweep it under the rug." Catastrophizing is a more exaggerated demonstration than magnification and is identified when people imagine a terrible outcome when what is experience is simply uncomfortable.

Moral reasoning

Moral reasoning can be another form of cognitive distortion. This does not refer to the level of moral development that you have achieved but rather the use of "should" statements that you impose on yourself or others irrespective of the parameters of the situation.

Examples of this kind of reasoning are when you hear people say, "You should do a, b, or c." Or when you hold certain expectations (shoulds) and get upset because those expectations are not met, often without understanding the reasons why they feel like they do.

Personalization

When a person attributes personal responsibility in a situation where he or she has no control. Often this is seen as egocentricity —"everything happens because of me"—like a young child.

This can be a more difficult one to ascertain as it depends on the beliefs regarding control. For instance, some people will claim that we have control over what we attract to us, whereas others will focus on what we do with a situation. There is a subtle difference between:

- Everything happens because of me.
- We are creating our life as we move through it.
- We are attracting situations to us because of underlying beliefs that direct our choices.

Depending on the attitude that comes with it, personalization may be the result of:

- Egocentricity, for example: A five-year-old may think his parents separated because of him when, in fact, it had nothing to do with him.
- New Age/Spiritual beliefs, such as, I am creating my lives as I move through it therefore I am responsible for everything that happens in my life.
- Psychological beliefs, such as, a woman keeps choosing an abusive husband because of underlying belief systems that she is not worthy *or* a sense of familiarity due to the abusive childhood that she had.
- Another psychological construct may be having been brought up with the belief always that you are responsible for making everything okay for everyone else, or that you are responsible for everyone's happiness.
- Believing that you are responsible for making relationships work.

With these types of messages, a child learns to be overly responsible for things that are not his or her responsibility.

Some will claim that our underlying life themes or past karma create our current situations, whereas others claim that we are constantly creating our path in life with our current beliefs and choices.

Blaming

Blaming is the opposite of personalization. It is identified as when a person *always* holds another responsible for whatever happens.

Now, this one can be difficult as well. For instance, divorce lawyers will tell you, they can usually tell (whether someone is their client or not) who is 40% to blame and who is 60% to blame for the discrepancies in the relationship. However, there are the odd cases when a lawyer will say "we will hold this person 5% responsible, because he/she is human and had to contribute something". Unfortunately, the one that is the major cause of the situation usually wants to focus on the 40/60 rule of thumb and has a total lack of awareness of what a mess he or she is creating.

Overgeneralization

Overgeneralization is another cognitive distortion. We often think of this as "Archie Bunker" thinking. Archie Bunker refers to a television show that ran in the 1970s. The reasoning is not limited to racial and gender issues but means that you generalize

So What's the Point?

within any given parameters and put all sharing those parameters into a box. This could be people within a certain occupation or profession, people with specific disabilities, weight issues, sexual orientations, or any other kind of parameter. Everyone with that character is thrown into the same group, which becomes overgeneralization.

Examples of this might be:

- All black people are inferior.
- All females are emotional.
- All police officers are controlling.
- All people with ADHD have lower intelligence.
- All people with weight issues eat too much.

Every one of the above generalizations is incorrect. Let's look at them individually.

If all blacks are inferior, then how do you explain that black people have succeeded in every profession and career? Black people can be warm, loving, affectionate, gentle people, just like every other people group.

If you assume that all females are emotional, how can you account for the ice maiden stereotype or the fact that many males have violent or uncontrollable tempers?

As a side note, because females tend to have a more developed left frontal lobe, they tend to have more effective communication skills. Thus, they have a greater capacity to articulate their emotions as opposed to males who are more known for their anger. Now note, I have used terms like "tend to", "known for", "well known" etc. – these are recognized tendencies, not absolutes.

If all police officers are controlling, how do we account for the police officer who is patient, kind, supportive, artistic, and more?

If all people with ADHD have lower intelligence, how do we account for the fact that when you eliminate the hyperactivity, about 60% of ADHDs actually have a near genius mentality?

If all people with weight issues eat too much, how do we account for the fact that there is a significant proportion of overweight people who don't eat enough?

Most people know and understand on some level that the reason that the first set of statements is wrong is because they do not hold true. There is a wide spectrum of people with varying characteristics, in any group of people.

The problem with overgeneralization is that hasty judgments or assumptions are made based on only a small amount of information.

Unfortunately, with over generalization, it only takes one or two with some negative characteristic, and the whole group is attributed that characteristic. This is what overgeneralization does.

Filtering

Filtering is another form of cognitive distortion based on too little information. An example of this when someone is given numerous positive complements but choose to focus on one criticism instead. People who tend toward this habit may also reflect another psychological construct, other validation versus self-differentiation. Most people live on the "other validation" end of this continuum. They allow people and events outside of themselves to determine their worth. A good extreme example of this was in the Stock Market Crash of 1929. Those who were caught up in other validation often committed suicide rather than suffer the shame of publicly acknowledging their losses. Those who had a greater sense of self-differentiation recognized the challenge of the moment, what they had lost, and then set out to rebuild their financial situation.

Negating the positive

Negating the positive is another form of cognitive distortion. Often religious constraints that we learned in the past dictate that we *should* not take credit for anything we do and that we need to minimize our contributions when others acknowledge us. If we are taught that if we take or accept credit for our achievements then we are arrogant, narcissistic or conceited, it becomes extremely difficult to accept a compliment. So we learn to discredit any acknowledgement and write it off as flattery, to minimize it, or to discredit it outright as opposed to acknowledging the compliment with grace and appreciation.

Perhaps a healthier way of looking at a compliment is with appreciation that the other person took the time to notice and say something. Respect and thank them for that rather than minimize what they had to say.

All of these cognitive distortions will affect why you ask the question, "so what's the point?" and also affect how you answer the question.

For instance, the person who comes from the place that he believes he is responsible for everything that happens in his life will have an entirely different reason for asking the question and an entirely different answer than the person who blames everything in her life on everyone else.

Likewise, the person who maximizes everything—makes a mountain out of a molehill—will have entirely different reasons and answers than the person who minimizes everything.

So What's the Point?

EXERCISE:

Which, if any, of the distortions identified above do you tend to engage in the most?

How does using this distortion affect the answer to the question: So what's the point?

Choose a cognitive distortion you don't usually utilize and ask why you would ask the question and how would you answer it.

If you could choose any cognitive distortion, which would you choose, and why?

How would your life change if you started using this cognitive distortion?

Can you imagine a life without any cognitive distortions—how would it be different?

Rather than change your style of operating, why not simply become aware of how you are operating?

CHAPTER 4

What about people who are not criminals but cause chaos for everyone else?

As much as most of us are aware of the chaos that criminals can cause, one doesn't have to be a criminal to cause chaos. Now, with this concept I am working the Western values here. I am not dealing with countries that allow for abuse of women and children or countries that throw people in jail for standing up for their rights or are willingly abuse, torture, and kill people who don't abide by the dictates of the ruling government.

This chapter is dealing with people who can cause chaos and misery to everyone around them. These are also people who get upset when you try to hold them accountable for the damage that they have done. These people seem to have no awareness of the hurt, pain, and loss that others have suffered because of their behaviour.

Or, what about people who are law-abiding citizens but who lie to themselves about themselves? They also lie to themselves about others, lie to the world about themselves, and lie to the world about others. They often know a higher moral yet choose to take a lower one.

On a more psychological level, lying to yourself about who you are and why you do what you do has an impact or a consequence for most of us. But it may have a very different impact for the person who has poor self-esteem or a poor self-identity or a person who is narcissistic or psychopathic.

Different psychological modalities will have different answers to the question, whether it be, humanistic psychology, spiritual psychology, positive psychology, cognitive behavioral psychology, (to name a few) but all explore the question "so what's the point?" from different perspectives. Rather than exploring how the different psychological perspectives address the question, we are going to explore how the question applies to different aspects of life.

Often people who make poor choices do not seem to have to pay for their poor choices. Others may protect them or enable them or rescue them. They don't seem to learn their lessons and they keep causing damage by blaming others for the damage done.

These types of people often cause us to ask what the point is? The point here might be about you are willing to do with it. Should you accept such individuals as they are? Or, do you need to erect better boundaries?

If you stop enabling or rescuing them, you may suffer again—perhaps only in the short term but possibly in the long term as well. If you hold such a person accountable, what do you do if they still refuse to accept responsibility for their actions? What do you do when you feel like you are banging your head against a stonewall and asking yourself, "What's the point?"

What are you doing with it? Is the saying, "Life is 10% what happens to you and 90% what you do with it," of value in this situation?

What if the person causing all the chaos is your child? What does love mean now? Can you:

- Continue to rescue?
- Continue to protect?
- Walk away?
- Allow them to find their bottom line?
- What if that means allowing them to end up on skid row?
- What if that means they end up in jail?
- What if that means they get involved with drugs?
- What if that means they turn to prostitution?

If this person is your child, what is the point in enabling him or her? What is the point in abandoning them?

EXERCISE:

Identify a situation in your life when you felt you were dealing with someone who just "didn't get it". What was your behavior? Your attitude?

Rather than focus on what they needed to learn, ask yourself what was the lesson you needed to learn?

Was it how to walk away?

Was it how to set more effective boundaries?

Did you learn to stop rescuing them or protecting his or her?

Do you have the courage to make it about you rather than them?

CHAPTER 5

Actions and Consequences

We have brought up the concept of action and consequences a few times. People struggle with their actions and the consequences of their actions for different reasons. Let's deal with this subject from a different perspective.

We tend to struggle with this for two reasons. One results from suffering from the actions of others. For example, if we believe we have made good choices and behaved well, and still end up suffering because of someone else's ignorance, judgments, actions, etc. we may ask, why me? Or, so what was the point?

If, on the other hand, we see individuals acting poorly, causing suffering to others, and they "get away with it" we may question why we bother to act with good conscience and high morals when others don't and it doesn't seem to matter. Let's look at both.

Let's deal with the first situation. People suffering at the hands of others due to greed, ignorance, power or control, etc. has plagued mankind throughout history. Extreme examples of this occur during wars, revolutions, with activists, etc. They occur when "distorted" peoples are in power, i.e. people who ran the "blood gold" tyrannies, or the Hitler regime, women and children who have been raped and ganged raped, and people are tortured. In some situations, the people who lead these horrific situations are:

- Psychopaths
- Sociopaths
- Mentally ill (delusional, paranoid, schizophrenic, etc.)
- Mentally ill (syphilis gone to the brain)

Sometimes their devotees follow them because they:

Don't know how to think for themselves:

- Need a leader
- Become swept up by peer pressure
- Need to belong to a group, or to feel accepted
- Live a life of guilt and shame over what they may have done

Regardless of why the leaders perpetrate these kinds of situations or why their followers will obey them, the victims have done nothing wrong, except be in the wrong place at the wrong time, yet they've suffered at the hands of others.

This kind of situation has occurred throughout history. People have been jailed, beheaded, or burned at the stake for having beliefs that differed from the status quo. Suggesting a different way of seeing things may provoke fear, competition, or a loss of control. For instance:

- When the belief that the earth was not the centre of the universe was challenged.
- When the belief that the world was not flat was challenged.
- When research challenged prevailing medical notions regarding bacteria, viruses, etc.
- If people believed anything other than existing church orthodoxy.
- When witches were burned at the stake for a wide variety of reasons.

In these cases, the victims simply abided by different beliefs and yet suffered horrifically at the hands of others.

This kind of injustice also occurs because of religious beliefs. People are willing, or are taught from a young age, to kill others or themselves, or to abuse others in the name of their religion, which can actually be about greed, power, and control. Again, the leaders and the followers may have different individual reasons but does that matter to the victim?

This kind of injustice also occurs in judicial systems. There are situations where those in control will abuse others, whether it is justified by establishing and maintaining control or for their own gratification. Or, they may try to cover up for what those in the judicial system are doing. There are a lot of reasons people inappropriately suffer at the hands of others in judicial systems.

Nelson Mandela and Hurricane (Rubin Carter) are well known examples of people who were not only jailed but kept in isolation for years. Yet Mandela went on to become the President of South Africa and Horizon was never guilty of the charges against him. What is particularly interesting about cases like these is how these individuals utilized their time to develop spiritually with awesome results.

We have heard of judges who have sexually abused teenage girls for decades and got away with it for decades before being caught, or lawyers and judges who have protected their involvement in illegal drug trafficking. Many situations in the judicial system expose the suffering of one to cover up for the sins of another.

Suffering at the hands of others also happens in less physically aggressive situations. For instance, look at the hold the pharmaceutical companies have over physicians, or the hold the governments have over vaccinations, or the hold the medical associations have over physicians who use alternative methods, or the hold any college board has over their registrants, etc. While these holds may not be physically aggressive, they can be very aggressive in other ways and the resulting anguish can cause all kinds of physical problems.

These kinds of holds are imposed for a variety of reasons. For instance, they may establish or maintain power. They may be utilized to protect the egos of those with conventional beliefs. This is often referred to as the "old boy's club". For these groups to allow for growth and change, new beliefs to integrate, etc. then they might have to:

- Question whether what they were doing was beneficial or detrimental.
- Review their careers from a different perspective.
- Give up control.
- Do research and expand their perspective.

These types of physically non-aggressive holds are what control the status quo and prevent mankind from moving forward. In hindsight, they are regarded with disbelief, yet they continue to perpetuate. Man often has a difficult time learning from past mistakes.

Throughout history people have suffered at the hands of others, predominantly because of ignorance, greed, and control. And so we can ask—what is the point of struggling to grow and expand when we are up against peoples who are in a position of power and operate out of ignorance, greed, control, fear of losing control, fear of the possible competition, or fear that they might be wrong?

When we have suffered at the hands of a person or a group, whether that group be a family group, a community group, or a political group, we may understand where they are coming from and believe it is about power, greed, fear, or ignorance, or we may not have a clue what we did to deserve such suffering. Either way, we might ask, "So what was the point?"

When we, or our loved ones, suffer because others act from a place of ignorance, greed, selfishness, or power, we have a difficult time dealing with it. When we see others acting from a place of selfishness and not caring about the impact they have on others, we have a difficult time dealing with it. When we see people act out of malice or vindictiveness, without vindication, we ask: So what's the point?

When we want actions to have consequences and we don't see that happening we often get angry and frustrated, or bitter and resentful. We may struggle, looking both at possible short-term consequences and long-term consequences to find the answers. Why do some appear to get their "karma" while others don't?

Why do some apparently get away with so much while others suffer so much for unknown reasons?

We also struggle with the other side of the problem. When we work hard and put a lot of effort into something that then goes wrong, what then? When someone else benefits from our efforts and we don't seem to, why is that? When we study hard and don't pass the exam, or practise hard and don't make the team, then what? When we pound the pavement and can't seem to get the job or the break; when we think we have tried our best and we are still frustrated with the outcome; when we have worked a lot harder than another and yet get less pay—why does this happen? There are a thousand different situations in life, where we put out a lot of effort and don't get the pay off or suffer because of someone else's choices; we ask, "What is the point?"

As many examples we have just listed, there are some answers to these questions, such as:

- You were in the wrong place at the wrong time.
- You were just born in the wrong place or at the wrong time.
- You attracted this situation to yourself from an underlying belief.
- You attracted this situation to yourself from a past life action, attitude, or belief.

So What's the Point?

- You attracted this situation to yourself from the choices you made in this life.
- There was an individual, group or racial karma that needed to be addressed, learned, or resolved.
- You were ahead of your time.
- You needed to learn about forgiveness and acceptance.
- The suffering provided you with an opportunity to develop spiritually.
- Mankind is cruel.
- You were able to help others learn.
- You needed something dramatic to help you to learn.

This is just a short list of possible explanations and not presented in any particular order. Depending on your level of growth—ego, moral, spiritual, you will come up with different answers along the way.

You have a choice here. Will you choose an answer that fits with your status quo (values, beliefs, attitudes, etc.) or will you choose an answer that pushes you towards greater growth, learning, and awareness, or your optimum potential?

EXERCISE:

Many see life as 'the workout gym' for the soul. When challenges happen, it is like your soul has gone to the gym for a workout to eliminate the excess weight, ideas, or attitudes and strengthen your muscles, faith, or your higher self.

1. Identify the best three times in your life. What learning did you get from them?

2. Identify the worst three times in your life. What learning did you get from them?

3. Typically, we find that when we had the most challenges, we also had the most opportunity to grow and learn.

4. Identify a time in your life when you didn't learn the lesson and life was kind and patient enough to give you the lesson again, perhaps in another form.

5. Identify a time in your life when you learned a concept but didn't integrate the lesson and again life was patient and kind and provided you with another lesson.

6. Identify a time in your life when you learned the lesson, integrated the lesson into how you operated, and never found yourself in that situation again.

7. Identify a time in your life when you learned the lesson, integrated the lesson into how you operated but did find yourself in a similar situation but with an entirely different attitude, belief, or reaction.

8. Identify a time in your life, or someone else's, that there does not appear to be an answer to why they are experiencing or have experienced the injustice in this life. How can you develop your belief system to account for this situation?

CHAPTER 6

Relationships—Is there a point?

Relationships can be fun or agonizing, and sometimes both. Some people will claim that you need to be in some kind of romantic relationship in order to do achieve the most growth and learning. Others will argue that you can grow and learn more on your own than when caught up in a relationship, just like the great masters and gurus, or nuns and monks.

This reminds me of the two different perspectives in Buddhism. One perspective is that you gain the most spiritual growth and development by living your life in service to others. This allows you to give up your ego and develop as a human being. The other perspective is that your growth and spiritual development is about you, not about others. Focus on the self, develop the self to your greatest potential and you will be in service to mankind. Both perspectives are possible. Again, life is about choices.

Some people will benefit more by being in a relationship and others will benefit more by being on their own. Similarly, some may hide from any growth and development by being in a relationship and others will hide from the growth and development by being on their own.

A relationship may provide you with a mirror to see yourself. It may provide experiences within which to understand yourself or provide challenges within which to observe the self.

Unfortunately, our school systems fail us dramatically when it comes to relationships. Let's look at a couple of reasons why:

We are taught twelve years of language arts but nowhere along the way are we taught to communicate effectively.

Relationships may not always require a lot of verbal communication but they require effective communication, such as:

- Are people aware of their tone and attitude when talking?
- Are people aware of the volume with which they talk?

Men are more often sensitive to women raising their voices in frustration and claim that "she is yelling", when in fact only her volume was raised. Often these same people are not aware of how loud their voice can get.

Are people aware that words not only have a dictionary meaning but also a connotative meaning, the meaning that was attributed to the words in their family or cultural environment?

General agreement is that about 90% of communication is non-verbal.

- Are people aware of their posturing while talking?
- Are people aware of their facial expression while talking?
- Are people aware of rolling their eyes or sighing or other non-verbal communications?

We are taught twelve years of mathematics and/or algebra but nowhere along the way are we taught to establish and follow a budget.

For years, I practiced as a psychologist and was always amazed at how often marital problems revolved around finances. There are three major features regarding finances and any one of them can be the cause of issues. These are:

- How we accumulate finances.
- How we identify with finances.
- How we disperse finances.

Sometimes the manner of accumulating finances can cause marital issues, such as:

How honorable or ethical is the manner of achieving finances?

How much time is spent accumulating finances?

So What's the Point?

Is the manner in which you accumulate finances perceived as of value by your partner?

How we identify with finances can also cause problems, like:

- Do you think finances give you power or control?
- Do you think finances give you value or make you important?
- Do you realize that the only thing finances give you is choices?

Sometimes the manner in which we choose to disperse finances can cause problems. These can include:

- If one person is a saver and the other is a spender.
- If one person is an impulsive buyer whereas the other is a strategist, i.e. will save to purchase a car or a house.

If one person purchases negative investments whereas the other purchases only positive investments.

If one person abides by a budget and the other hasn't a clue how to budget or how to abide by it.

We are taught many years of social studies and history but nowhere along the way are the taught to learn from both our own experiences and the experiences of others. A relationship may require you to:

- Set better boundaries.
- Take others into consideration.
- Accept others.
- Give more than you receive.
- Listen well.
- Share.
- Trust others.
- Compromise.
- Ask for what you need.
- Be responsible to and for others.
- Come from the heart.
- Be patient.
- Learn to move from "infatuation to love to being loving.

However, if you are on your own, you may be able to create more time and pay more attention to developing and understanding the self without other distractions. Being on your own may require you to:

- Be self-sufficient.
- Be independent.
- Be your own comforter.
- Be self-fulfilled.

So What's the Point?

- Find your true source of happiness.
- Be responsible to the self.
- Focus on your own growth and development.
- Love and accept the self.
- Be good to yourself.
- Develop self-discipline.
- Develop self-initiative.
- Develop self-value.
- Trust yourself.

Regardless of which way you choose to operate at this point, let's look at romantic or sexual relationships. You may choose a relationship for a variety of poor reasons, such as:

- To get out of an abusive home life.
- Because you are tired of being alone.
- To get the love you felt you never had.

Because you believe you should (family, peer, social expectations).

- Because of pressure (from partner, family, friends).
- Because of convenience (accommodations, finance, children).
- Because of a pregnancy.
- Because of romanticized, idealized beliefs.
- To have a stable sexual relationship.

- Because you find someone with whom you have a lot of things in common.
- Because you are a rescuer and you are rescuing someone.
- Because you are a controller and you can control this person.
- Because you are co-dependent.

If you are truly fortunate, you will commit to a relationship because you truly love the other person and this other person truly loves you. However, loving does not guarantee a healthy relationship. Regardless of the reasons you choose to commit to a relationship, there are many issues that can make that relationship a success, a good challenge, or a disaster.

First let's look at a couple of issues that can make the relationship both a wonderful success and a good challenge.

Healthy marriages (or a committed relationship) have a competitive component to them.

Most people raise their eyebrows when I say this. But let's walk through it and understand why, rather than just negate it. Can you imagine a relationship wherein each person was committed to making the other feel the most loved and special for the rest of his or her lives? That is a good healthy competition. What if each person was committed to accepting the other as he or she currently is and to supporting the other in achieving his or her optimal potential.

We have another good healthy competition.

This doesn't come easily for most people. To achieve this, both partners must be committed to:

- Listening to and understanding the other person's needs and challenges and knowing when and how to meet them.
- Recognizing when the spouse or partner needs just to be heard or needs help.
- Understanding how and when the other feels the most loved and special.

Notice how each of the categories listed below, have a number of different expressions. It is not only important to understand the category but which type of expression within that category means something to the other person. Another component may be about frequency – is it enough to know it once a year, once a month, once a week, or on a daily basis? It is also important to come to terms with what is being ridiculous, needy, or just a need. Let's look at some commonly recognized categories, starting with acts of affection:

- Holding hands.
- Massaging each other's feet/shoulders.
- Cuddling on the couch.
- Greeting each other when they come through the door.
- Kissing or holding hands publicly.
- Affectionately touching each other as they each move around the house.
- Hugging just for the sake of hugging.
- Kissing just for the sake of kissing.
- Sensual experiences include such activities as:
- Taking showers or baths together.
- Body massages.

Sexual experiences can take place:

- In the bedroom.
- In the kitchen.
- In the shower.

Acts of service that couples can do for each other include:

- Housecleaning
- Laundry
- Cooking
- Making the beds
- Cleaning up after yourself

- Yard work or gardening
- Mowing the lawn
- House maintenance/repair
- Car maintenance/repair
- Looking after finances

Gift giving is also an important part of successful relationships and can take the form of:

- Gifts you made yourself
- A thoughtful gift you picked up on the way from work
- A card or flower
- A special cup of coffee
- Something that you heard your mate express a wish for that you took the time to listen and go and get it
- Something expensive
- Something just because as opposed to a particular occasion

Love and affection can also be expressed in quality time spent:

- By yourself
- Taking a bath
- Time to just sit and read
- Time to meditate

- Time for the self
- Going to the gym, working out
- Walking, biking, running
- Time to spend any way you want to
- Time with your partner
- In quiet time together
- Time together talking
- Time together working on the house or garden
- In social time with the partner
- Time with immediate family (children)
- Time with extended family
- Time with friends but not family
- Time with friends and family

Words of validations (this can be difficult if the other person expects words of validation yet has done nothing to earn them).

- Validating how good a spouse they are
- Validating how good a parent they are

Acknowledging and appreciating how much time and effort he or she has put out:

- Validating his or her looks
- Validating his or her skills or abilities
- Validating his or her home

So What's the Point?

- Acknowledging your love for him or her

Understanding what support means to another person, which could include:

- Listening
- Supportive words
- Their own quiet time
- You taking care of the children
- Just being still with them
- Affection
- Confirming that everything will be all right

You would think that when our needs are all met, and people have no complaints that people would *not* ask what the point is but that is not the case. Many times, people start asking this question because they are bored, because there are struggling to push us to the next step in life. It is an important question that can motivate us to look deeper and wider, to grow and learn, and to develop greater awareness.

Some will blame relationships, while others will conclude that they were not cut out for being a parent or a spouse. Some may decide that they missed out on youth. When people find life unfulfilling, they can adopt any of the cognitive distortions listed earlier to justify leaving a relationship and looking for fulfillment elsewhere. The question that usually comes up becomes, is that all there is? Unfortunately, the real problem may arise from:

- Inability to find happiness within
- Internal drive for further growth and development
- Inability to appreciate what they have
- Inability to achieve self-fulfillment

Leaving a relationship will not in and of itself solve most personal problems. The may find a temporary Band-Aid™ solution but when it falls off the underlying problem will still be there. Some will develop addictions in order to avoid dealing with deeper problems and others they will go from relationship to relationship always looking for answers in someone else. Will they recognize that they need to find the answers within and actually start looking there?

Another cause of problems in relationships that will provoke people to ask what the point can be a result of the following three styles of relationships:

1) Two givers who operate with the theme: Give more than you take this is the healthiest of relationships.

2) Two takers who operate with the theme: Get as much as you can and don't worry about what you give in return.

So What's the Point?

> This is going to be a relationship about negative competition.

3) One person who is a giver and one person who is a taker. This relationship is going to be abusive—physical, sexual, and/or verbal abuse can result. Other forms of abuse, victimization, or imbalance may include when one partner perceives him- or herself as doing all the work in the relationship.

I know of one case where the husband was self-employed and brought in all the finances but also did the majority of housecleaning, washed and ironed his own clothes, and did the majority of cooking. They had no children so there was no parenting. Despite his contributions to the relationship the woman was verbally abusive and demanding.

Imbalance in relationships occurs when:

- One partner perceives the other is living off the rewards he/she has created
- One partner perceives him- or herself as contributing more than the other, whether that be time, money, or effort.
- One partner works hard at creating a good relationship while the other is willing to reap the

benefits but doesn't appear to put in any effort.

- One partner believes he or she is a good partner but discovers that the other is having an affair with someone else.
- One partner needs more affection than the other is willing to give.
- One partner needs more quality time than the other is willing to give.
- One partner needs more words of validation that the other is willing to give. This may also be the case where the husband and wife work together.

People in any of the above situations may feel, and actually, be victimized. People who are victimized in relationships should ask the question why they remain in the situation as it stands. Psychologically, the more important issue here is whether the victimized person operates like a victim. One may be victimized without operating like a victim, whereas another may identify with their victimization. If you believe that you are being targeted but are doing something about it then you are not a victim. You may be survivor or you may go even further and be a thriver. If you make the shift internally, the rest will follow.

What do you need to do in your relationship? Do you need to learn to:

- Set better boundaries?
- Be able to say no?
- Be able to walk away and say, "enough is enough"?
- Recognize how they might be provoking the problem?
- Recognize that they might be enabling the problem?
- Recognizing that they are *not* to blame for another's inadequacies?

Recognize that they may be suffering from victimization because of:

- Underlying life themes, i.e. they are not worthy or lovable, or that do not deserve any better, or that women are meant to be abused, etc.
- Underlying value systems, i.e. it is more important to stay and suffer than to abandon another, or that they will get to heaven if they continue to forgive and be patient, etc.
- Underlying fears like, fear of being on one's own, fear of not being able to provide for children, fear of the unknown.

- Underlying beliefs, such as, "you made your bed, now lie in it", "suffer in silence", "everyone else is suffering behind closed doors as well".

EXERCISES:

If you are not in a relationship, this chapter may not apply to you. However, if you have left a relationship, you may need to utilize this chapter well, in order not to repeat the mistakes that were made in attracting a partner, developing a relationship with a chosen partner, or creating a relationship that is effective for you.

1. Identify why you want to be in a relationship.

2. Identify why you want this particular relationship.

3. Identify what you love most about your partner.

4. Identify what you need in a relationship. Now identify what your partner needs in a relationship.

5. Identify how and when you feel loved and special. Now identify how and when your partner feels loved and special.

6. Identify how often you feel loved and special. Now identify how often your partner feels loved and special.

7. Define what love means to you. Now identify what love means to your partner.

8. Balance can look very different in different relationships, for example:

- We each do 50% of the laundry.
- He takes care of the outside; I take care of the inside.
- I do the housecleaning; he takes care of the cooking.
- We split the mortgage 50/50 OR in ratio to our income.
- He works and she raises the kids.
- I take care of the finances and she gives me sex.

The point here is whether you both feel that there is a good balance. The balance may shift according to circumstances, but again do both of you feel there is a good balance.

9. Now have your partner do the exercise and compare your answers.

CHAPTER 7

What is the point of suffering?

For most people there has been a time in their life when they found life's journey extremely challenging. For some, life appears to be more challenging than for others or perhaps challenging more often than it is for others. While in the depths of our challenges, we often ask ourselves, what's the point?

We can't help but ask what a victim did to deserve when a drunken driver hits an innocent victim, or a serial killer attacks blameless people, or a pedophile violates innocent children.

We have questioned the horrors of the world from a different perspective earlier in the book. When innocent lives are taken in a drug war, a political war, or a religious war, we ask, "What was the point?" Most wars are fought for a variety of reasons. All have ego, power, and greed as the primary motivating forces regardless of the banner they use to convince their people to fight.

There are other kinds of victimization, too. What about when nature exerts power? Hurricanes, volcanoes, earthquakes, or tidal waves, can affect thousands of lives. When famine and disease run

So What's the Point?

through a country like Ethiopia, or AIDs affects millions in Africa, we may also question, "What is the point?"

When these natural disasters hit other countries and effect people we may not even know, it is easier to:

- Ignore the situation.
- Just feel a moment of sorrow for what they are going through and move on.
- Contribute to the cause financially and move on.
- Actively raise funds to help.
- Watch with interest but do nothing.

The closer to home these events occur, the greater the actual impact on us, and the more likely we are to question and search for answers.

These are hard questions to answer. For many, the questions and the search for answers is too overwhelming and they will not engage in the process, as a means of self-protection, or simply because they do not care, or are too overwhelmed with their own lives.

For those who do search for meaning and purpose in the events that occur in life, again we can come up with a variety of potential answers:

- In the wrong place at the wrong time
- Group karma
- The earth is clearing itself
- Suffering makes you stronger

Alternatively, you may want to hold the people who suffered accountable. They should have listened to the reports and moved out. Why do they live in an area that is prone to disaster?

But we may also want to ask bigger questions, such as:

1. Why do we need to suffer?

2. Why does God allow us to suffer? Does God not care?

3. Is suffering our punishment for being human?

4. Why did someone else die and I am still alive?

5. In the case of a child suffering, what was the point of being born if you are just going to suffer a horrible death and not even get to live life?

6. Is this due to some karmic debt or lesson?

Tough questions.

EXERCISE:

1. Identify what your beliefs are regarding why people suffer due to natural disasters or car accidents, etc.

2. Identify whether your beliefs would change if you knew people who were caught in the disaster. For example, what if the people caught in the disaster were family or friends of yours.
3. Identify what your actions would be in both cases, i.e. the known versus the unknown.
4. Identify which bigger question is most important to you and why.

Now you know there is no absolute answer to any particular question but you can find answer that will work for you right now.

CHAPTER 8

Why do we compare?

Very often we look for meaning when we don't appear to be getting as good a deal as someone else. This of course requires comparing our lives, our efforts, or our suffering to someone else's.

We learn to compare from a very young age. Parents will get younger children to look at older children's behavior as a reference for what to do. Or they will find a person in the extended family or neighborhood that they want the child to emulate, if they are not pleased with the child's behavior.

The media teaches us from a young age to compare our toys with someone else's, as if that is how we are to determine our value. In school, we learn to compare our worth as a student by how our marks compare with those of others. Thus, we learn to compare. We learn to judge both good and bad. We determine what we want to be through comparison to others. Who is cool, who is smart, who is responsible, and who is successful. We also learn to judge who is bad, who is not in the "in crowd", who is irresponsible and who is a "loser".

So What's the Point?

Thus we tend to compare our situation with three groups of people:
- Those around us
- Those at the "perceived top"
- Those perceived to be or have less than us

We do these comparisons for different reasons. The most predominant reason is to give us value. We often look at those around us to see if we are keeping up, i.e. "with the Joneses". Do they have more or less than we have? Do they have something we want?

Media, in western society, has taught us to value ourselves in terms of what we have. This shallow and empty way of believing we are of value keeps our economy going. Thus, we live in a very materialistic world. While we like to think that most of *know* that stuff does not give us value, enough people have bought into the belief, enough of the time, to keep this materialistic economy going.

Another common way for western society to determine value is through presentation. Thus, we have the fashion industry. Buying the latest shade, or designer name, or style drives the fashion industry, therefore, the fashion industry is a huge component of today's retail market.

Up until the 1960s people tended to buy children clothing on three occasions, if they were lucky: with each new school year, at Christmas, and on a birthday. There simply wasn't extra money to purchase items between these occasions. You were very appreciative if you got items on these occasions. Furthermore, these exciting gifts were often socks and underwear, or whatever was needed.

By the 1970s the clothing market started to push seasonal purchases. By the 1990s there were mid-season shifts in colors, tones, etc. In today's world of consumerism, the purchase market is constant. One must keep up, and therefore, one must purchase regularly to feel of value, if you are willing to "buy" into that concept—and most are.

Cosmetics and cosmetic surgery accounts for millions of dollars spent every year in North America. Again, another big industry where the advertising goal is to communicate that your value comes from looking as good as, if not better, than the next person. This advertising premise usually means looking young, slim, and beautiful. Naturally, gym memberships and gym equipment sales play the same propaganda.

The second group of people that we tend to compare ourselves with is those we want to emulate. In Western society this may begin at a young age and the focus will usually be on people in the entertainment field, i.e. musicians and/or actors and/or athletes who have "made it big". However, many recognize that power, fame, and wealth do not equate to value, meaning, and purpose and they are left asking the question, "So what's the point?"

There is, however, a smaller but significant population who will choose other people to emulate. For instance, some children will choose a teacher, a religious character, or a scientist. They will choose to emulate someone who has made a big impact on them for reasons other than fame and money. Many will look to leader such as Gandhi, Nelson Mandela, or the Dalai Lama. Or perhaps in business, to people like Muhammad Yunas, the man who founded the Grameen Bank, who have made a profound impact on the lives of others and creating changes that benefit the greater good of all.

Studies from different cultures around the world repeatedly show that when people strive for self-development they find more happiness and satisfaction in their lives than those who seek fame, greed, and power. Theories of self-actualization present stages of development in life. Many psychologists, like Abraham Maslow, recognized that when our basic needs of safety, shelter, food, and belonging were met, we then move towards self-actualization. Some people will work towards self-actualization without even recognizing it. Others will do it with conscious intent; others get stuck in their world of familiarity and complacency and never move towards their greater potential. When get stuck is when we ask the question, "So what's the point?"

The more common trend among the general population, however, is to choose someone who is famous and wealthy to emulate. There is a general belief that these people have more value. This person/group then becomes the icon to follow after and strive towards. This continues until a child/teen/adult reaches an age whereby they realize that it takes a lot more work and effort than they are willing to put out.

They are left interpreting the world, and the value therein, through the lens of fame, power, and greed, as if this gives their life value, purpose, and meaning. This continues until they realize that fame, power, and greed do not fill the inner void or give life meaning.

The third group of people that we tend to compare ourselves with are those who are less fortunate than we are. Most of the time, people in first world countries forget to take into consideration the fact that two-thirds of the world's people are starving to death, living in war torn countries, or are poverty-stricken because of drought and other economic or natural situations.

So What's the Point?

In first world countries, people can also grow up with physical, sexual, verbal or emotional abuse, and many children are nutritionally starved or grow up with neglect, negation, or other forms of negativity.

If a natural disaster is broadcasted, such as when a tsunami hits or a volcano erupts or a hurricane strikes, we "feel" for these people who have less than we do or who are suffering, as we are not. The comparisons tend to last as long as the broadcasts do and then take a huge drop. We easily forget the sufferings of others but while the suffering is being broadcasted, we are often besieged with the question concerning, "What is the point?"

When we compare ourselves to those less fortunate than ourselves at home, the impact will tend to be directly proportional to the personal contact. For some, these situations may offer an immediate sense of value as someone is worse of than themselves.

Very often we hear, we "should not" compare ourselves to others. What makes that an important statement? Why is it both correct and wrong at the same time? All three of these questions need to address the same issue: What is the intent?

Learning to look at one's intentions is a big component of psychology. What is driving behavior?

For example, what about murder? Was a death caused with malicious, vindictive intent? Or was the death caused by accident, i.e. a car accident. Or was the death caused as a side effect of protecting someone else, i.e. protecting a child.

If the intent behind "comparing" is to set up a goal to work towards then it could be a good aim. If the goal is to simply gain money, fame, or power then it will turn out to be a hollow goal because the objective was ultimately selfish and it will leave a void to be filled through other means.

A complex intent might be a goal that on the surface appears to be driven by good intentions but with only a little bit of exploration, it turns out to be a negative intent, i.e. giving to charity because it made you look good or was a great tax write-off.

Perhaps this is one reason why some people who are famous and/or wealthy end up with drug and alcohol problems. The goal was to attain external value in terms of fame and wealth without developing the self and as such, did not fill the void inside. In fact, it may have just emphasized the hole inside.

Sometimes, however, the inability to handle the fame and fortune is a result of not having time to develop a solid sense of self first. The fame and fortune become enmeshed with the self-identity, and the person no longer knows who they are apart from the superficial.

So What's the Point?

The extent to which the goal of comparison is striving to be a better person in some way, it will be a fulfilling intention. Most of us know, without the necessity of the growing amount of research available, that when people strive to better themselves or to make the world a better place, they end up feeling good inside. In both the subjective and the objective research, people rate higher on scales of happiness, satisfaction in life, and contentment, when they are working towards making themselves and the world a better place.

If, on the other hand, the goal of the comparison is negative, i.e. make an excuse for yourself, victimize yourself, blame yourself, or to be of either more or less value than another, you will not find happiness, satisfaction, or contentment.

I have yet to meet someone in therapeutic practice or in my private life wherein comparisons driven by a negative intent have any positive or beneficial outcome. Comparisons driven by negative intent leave people unfulfilled, empty, and unhappy. When people find themselves in this place they either try desperately to fill the void using various addictions or in despair ask, "What is the point?"

On the other hand, if the negative intent is utilized well to motivate one to do something different, then the "simple negative intent" becomes a "complex negative intent" and it can have positive value. For instance, if I were to compare myself negatively and blame myself for not achieving something I saw someone else achieve, and used that to motivate myself to achieve the goal, then through complex negative intent I could achieve something that gave me fulfillment.

EXERCISE:

1. To whom do you compare yourself and why?
2. Name the top five people you admire the most (alive, dead or fiction).
3. Name the top five characteristics you admire the most about these people.
4. How many of these characteristics describe you?

CHAPTER 9

What about when we try hard without achieving what we are struggling for in business?

This is a common problem. We struggle hard to achieve something, such as a job or occupation, a trade or profession, self-employment, an ability to do a sport, play an instrument, or dance and sing.

People may give up in frustration when they don't seem to be going anywhere and end up asking, "So what's the point?"

People may tell you:

- Success is just around the corner
- People who are determined will eventually succeed
- About people who struggled and did succeed.

I am providing the following list – not because you need to read all of them to get the message but because it is so motivating to read how many people, persisted at huge costs, and did make it. The following is just a short list of a few examples in a few different areas. Now, I have also presented some personal examples, just to show, that the successes don't have to be huge to be meaningful to you.

Business:

Walt Disney, who went bankrupt three times before making it, is rumored to have received 302 rejections for financing loans for Disney World. And a new editor apparently fired him because he lacked imagination!

Colonel Sanders (Kentucky Fried Chicken) was rejected an acclaimed 1009 times before selling his chicken recipe, at sixty-five years of age, while driving around the country and sleeping in his car, wearing his famous white suit.

I was told repeatedly, it would take three good years to set up a private psychology practice of twenty client hours per week. I was doing thirty-six client hours a week within six months.

Whether big or small, don't depend on what "they" say to dictate your life. Learn what you can and then go on to create your own history.

Authors:

Jack Canfield, author of Chicken Soup for the Soul went to twenty-seven publishers before finding the one who made him famous.

So What's the Point?

Theodor Seuss Giesel, author of the Dr. Seuss books, was also rejected by twenty-seven publishers and now every child knows of Dr. Seuss.

John Grisham, another American author, (although first a lawyer) improved the negative probabilities. He was rejected twenty-eight times then went on to sell his first book, "A Time to Kill" for five thousand dollars. Now he has sold over 250 million copies of his books

Steven King's book, Carrie, was rejected thirty times. He ended up throwing it in the garbage but his wife rescued it and encouraged him to keep trying. He has now sold over 350 million copies.

Stephanie Meyer is an example of how not all authors follow the same path. She got her idea for the *Twilight* series from a dream and finished writing it in three months. From the fifteen submissions to literary agents, five didn't reply, nine rejected her story then eight publishers vied at auction for the rights to publish it.

Twelve publishers rejected J.K. Rowling, author of the Harry Potter collection, who apparently is now richer than the Queen of England. The one that gave her a chance told her to get a day job because there was no money in children's books. I love her quote to the Harvard 2008 graduating class:

"You might never fail on the scale I did," Rowling explained. "But it is impossible to live without failing at something, unless you live so cautiously that you might as well not have lived at all—in which case, you fail by default.

And here is a simple personal example. My father told me for years that I should write a book. I just couldn't see myself doing that. I didn't like writing. Writing my thesis for different degrees was an exercise that I didn't want to have to repeat. Then blogging came along and I found that I loved writing. After that, I started writing books on health and eleven titles have now been published.

You may not be a Walt Disney or a Steven Spielberg but engage and explore what your boundaries are, and if you choose, push farther.

Education:

Albert Einstein was rejected from university on the grounds he had no promise. He didn't speak until the age of four and didn't read till the age of seven—good lessons for both parents and teachers—yet he won the Nobel Price for modern physics.

Both my husband and I were told by the same Grade Eleven Physics teacher, four years apart, that he give us each a passing grade if we promised never to take physics again. Both of us agreed and passed. Both took physics in university and got A's.

Steven Spielberg's example is one I particularly like. He applied for and was rejected twice by the prestigious University of Southern California Film School. So he went to Cal State University instead. After directing some of the biggest movie blockbusters, and worth over $3 billion, he got an honorary degree from the very university that rejected him.

I was born with a genetic disorder, went through childhood with epilepsy, ADD (attention deficient disorder) and dyslexia (particularly with numbers). One neurologist told my family that people with my genetic disorder usually didn't finish high school and were typically dead by the age of twenty-five. I not only finished high school but have an Honors BA, two MAs, and am working on a second PhD. I also have several designations and am well past the age of twenty-five. This is my twelfth book, and I have another ten book outlines I am working on.

Again, don't allow others to limit your life. You decide where you want your boundaries to be, and then push them farther.

Artists:

Vincent van Gogh, the famous painter, sold only one of his eight hundred paintings in his lifetime, to a friend. Now they are in demand the world over and with his most expensive painting valued at $142.7 million!

On the music front, The Beatles, were rejected by various record labels. One famous rejection from a record label said: "guitar groups are on their way out" and "the Beatles have no future in show business."

My personal example here reflects how we can create our own limitations. I can remember in Grade Two having to make out of clay something in art class. I struggled to create a variety of things but nothing turned out the way I wanted it to. I ended up making an ashtray for my father for Father's Day. By the time Father's Day came, my father had quit smoking! I was proud of him. However, I had decided I was not creative and avoided all creativity from that point on.

One day, some forty years later, while on a vacation with an artist friend in Costa Rica, I borrowed one of her artist's pads and pencils. I went outside and drew the landscape. On the hill below me was a condo development of homes for vacationing peoples – all with difficult roof lines, beyond were the flowering trees and beaches that led out to the ocean. Surrounding the area were beautiful mountains. I found that I actually had a very good creative capacity and my friend was amazed. "I thought you said you couldn't draw. That is excellent!" she told me.

So What's the Point?

No, I did not make millions, nor do I sell any artwork but I learned a valuable lesson. We often limit ourselves without realizing our capabilities.

Whether knowingly or not, most people abide by an old Japanese proverb: "Fall down seven times, get up eight." It is interesting that we actually learn this lesson in our first year of life, as we literally learn to walk. We then apply it in a multitude of ways from learning to talk, to read and write, or to play catch.

On the other hand, many continue to apply the lesson but with ineffective attitudes such as anger, resentment, bitterness, or resignation.

So what's the point of this discussion?

1. The point is that there is no success without failure.
2. Failure may mean the choice not to try again or not to get up again
3. Failure may also mean the refusal to engage or to attempt
4. Failure may also mean the inability or the awareness to learn from your past challenges
5. Failure may also mean allowing others to dictate your life rather than engaging and establishing your own rules

Again, you have choices to make:

- How important is the challenge to you?
- Is it worth engaging in and risking rejection or failure?
- What does failure meant to you?

Everyone has people in his or her life who are more that willing to advise you:

- To quit
- To say "enough is enough"
- You are never going to make it
- You don't have enough talent, skill, ability

These are equally important concerns. So the old rule applies: "If you think you can, you can. If you think you can't, you can't."

Others may wonder, and feel compelled to question, whether you have enough:

- Self discipline
- Emotional stability
- Knowledge
- Skill for marketing

Perhaps you don't have these characteristics developed and you should start working on these characteristics first. Just become these characteristics don't come naturally to you, or perhaps you have not taken the time to develop them, doesn't prevent you from developing them now. It is simply a choice you make.

Perhaps the challenge for you isn't whether you have tried hard enough, or long enough but rather, have you been creative enough? Have you stepped outside of the box and attempted to market, connect, or achieve whatever you are struggling to accomplish, in a different way?

Maybe, you are seeking:

- The wrong target population. If you don't know how to identify your target population, there is a multitude of programs, individuals, or companies that can help you identify your target audience.
- The wrong kind of investors. There is a wide assortment of investors out there. Learn how to access them.
- The wrong kind of publisher. Today there is a variety of ways to self-publish, such as online publishing programs that will take you from an idea to full marketing.

- An ineffective marketing strategy. There are many individuals, companies, and programs that can help you organize the best strategy for your purposes.

When asking, "What's the point?" the answer may be in recognizing your:

- Limited vision
- Limited creativity
- Limited strategies
- Limiting beliefs on about your abilities
- Limiting beliefs about finances
- Limiting beliefs about success

EXERCISE:

If money and time were of no concern, what would you be doing? Make a list of five things. Then ask yourself:

1. How can you change that into an occupation? Be creative.
2. What is stopping you from doing that? Be honest.
3. What skills do you have to achieve that? Be realistic.
4. What characteristics do you need to work on that will help you? Be pragmatic.

5. Who do you need, to do what, to help you achieve your goals? Don't worry about the finances.
6. Now what is your first step?

CHAPTER 10

What about when we are struggling with weight issues without success?

Health is fundamental to good life. Many acclaim that without health, you have nothing or that health is your wealth. I look at this a bit differently. Whatever your state of health is, it is an opportunity for growth and development and an increased level of awareness.

For many in today's Western society, their health is about their weight. Tons of money is spent on weight issues every year on:

- Fad diets
- Supplements
- Gyms memberships
- Gym apparatus

All this is done in an attempt to counteract an ever-growing number on the scale. How many times have I heard people say things like, "I have tried everything and can't seem to lose weight"? Let me assure, it has happened many times.

So What's the Point?

We hear about the newest and greatest diet, supplement, herb, or exercise program touted as the be all and end all—the only solution you'll need to succeed.

So what do we say to the person who thinks that they have tried everything, they exercise, and diet, and they take supplements? We all know that what works for one doesn't necessarily work for another. We know there are all kinds of reasons for that from the physiological to the psychological.

Physiological causes can include:

- Deficiencies or inappropriate gut microbiota ratios
- Deficient enzymes
- Acidic pH
- Adrenal issues
- Liver issues
- Thyroid issues (which more often than not stem from adrenal issues)
- Heavy metal toxicity
- Other toxicities: POPs, PCBs, etc.
- Allergies
- Genetic disorders
- Mineral deficiency
- Glutathione deficiency

- Nutrition deficiency
- Eating too much
- Eating too little
- Eating foods that are working against you
- Lack of effective movement. The movement doesn't have to be workouts, lifting weights, etc. just good movements such as walking, biking, yoga, and Tai Chi.

Psychological causes could include:

- Underlying beliefs about self that stem from childhood
- Underlying beliefs about weight that stem from childhood
- Underlying life theme about shame, guilt, not being good enough
- Emotional eating habits, such as when upset, bored, frustrated, etc.
- Self-protection from life, from a parent, from a partner/relationship
- Eating out of habit rather than because you are hungry
- Eating reflects a psychological issue of "holding on"

So What's the Point?

If you have a weight problem, or know of someone who has, the driving factor may be any combination of the issues above. It is rarely just one.

While not about weight, I am going to share another story that may reflect an important possible answer. I was born with a genetic disorder. I don't make the same neurotransmitters, hormones, and enzymes as most people do. I grew up having seizures and other challenges as mentioned earlier in the book.

My parents diligently tried a variety of different treatments to stop the seizures. My mother, who only had a Grade 13 education, would go to medical conferences struggling to learn and understand what was going wrong and how to resolve the problem.

For two years, my parents diligently took me to an acupuncturist on a weekly basis to eliminate the seizures and while acupuncture works great for some types of seizures, it didn't work for me. Then they took me to a reflexologist for another two years, on a weekly basis. That didn't work either. They took me to a naturopath who put me on a 500-calorie diet for six months. I abided by it strictly yet it only made matters worse and and further altered my metabolism. Along the way we tried the Edgar Cayce remedies, behavioral techniques; anything and everything that anyone suggested, we tried.

Along the way, I was taking increasingly greater doses of more and more pharmaceutical medications. They only seemed to make matters worse. My mother kept charts of the petite mal seizures, the myoclonic seizures, and the grand mal seizures. She showed them to the neurologist and demonstrated how the seizures increased each time he put me on higher doses of medications. He would simply add another drug to the pile.

On one medication alone, I gained eighty pounds in six months and I am only five feet tall! During that time, I was put on several other medications as my system continued to shut down, organ by organ. I kept telling the neurologists, it's this one medication. They didn't believe me. I finally took myself off the drug.

I took 1600 mg/day of another medication for eight years. Several years later, they realized that you should never be on more than 600 mg/day (60% less than what I was taking) and for no longer than 2 years. I had been taking it for 8 years! A list of twenty-four major symptoms was put together that indicated whether or not a patient was toxic on the medication. I had twenty-two of the symptoms. One affect of the drug created problems in the metabolic system that couldn't be corrected. My metabolic system was already challenged way before the neurologists got involved.

So What's the Point?

I had various special weight trainers both from the university and privately and no one could understand why my body was not cooperating with the theories of the day.

Along the way, I learned how to meditate. Once I started meditating, by golly, the seizures stopped. With the increasing ability to calm down my own brain, I was able to eliminate the seizures.

So what is my point? Although there is a weight component tied up in the story, it was ultimately about the seizures. Just because one method doesn't work, don't stop exploring other possibilities. Sometimes, we can attempt a variety of different protocols:

- Medications
- Diets
- Exercise
- We can try different healing modalities:
  - Conventional
  - Alternative
  - Herbal
  - Homeopathic
  - Naturopathic
  - Ayurvedic
  - Traditional Chinese Medicine

We can try different exercise programs:

- Yoga
- Palletes
- Tai Chi
- QiGong
- Walking
- Biking
- Cardio

My point is, just because one thing or ten things don't work, don't stop exploring. Sometimes, the learning is tied up in the process of exploring the possibilities. You might be wise enough to be aware of the lessons you are learning in the process. You might be like most of us and see the lessons in retrospect. There are so many issues that contribute to weight management and you may need to develop a lot of patience.

Sometimes, along the way you learn lessons you might not otherwise have learned. Sometimes, it is your awareness that develops, or your open-mindedness. Sometimes you get to develop your diligence and determination. You may need to develop self-acceptance. You may need to let go of shame, guilt, or self-deprecation. Who knows what all the underlying possibilities might be? Keep moving forward. Be creative. Don't let one wall stop you. Don't get stuck; keep moving.

EXERCISE:

1. Identify your goal.
2. List the number of methods you have tried successfully.
3. List the number of methods you have tried unsuccessfully.
4. List the number of lessons you have learned along the way.
5. Now try combining working on a given lesson with a given weight loss method.

You may also want to read my book on Weight Management as it may give you some ideas you were not aware of before.

CHAPTER 11

What about when we are struggling for our health without apparent success?

Health—what a huge topic! We live in a time when so many of our foods are toxic or nutrient-deficient. We eat foods that are:

- Grown in toxic soils, bred in toxic waters, developed in toxic laboratories
- Artificial, microwaved, pasteurized, and processed
- Sprayed with toxic chemicals like Round Up and other POPs, PCBs, insecticides, and herbicides
- Injected with artificial hormones to provoke unnatural growth and weight gain; stained with colorants and sprayed with preservatives
- GMO (genetically modified organisms)
- Loaded with artificial and natural flavorings (usually as toxic as the artificial flavorings)
- Loaded with fillers that are GMOs
- Loaded with processed and artificial sugars and sweeteners

And we wonder why we are so sick.

So What's the Point?

But let's not forget that our water is also acidic and full of toxins. Our personal hygiene products and household cleaning products are also full of toxic chemicals.

When your body can no longer provide any more means of compensation and you start having symptoms you can go to your local MD and take some toxic medication that will hide the symptoms but not resolve the underlying issues.

Knowing all of that, one might ask: So what's the point? Good question. The point might be to step back and look at what you are…

- putting into your mouth
- rubbing onto your skin
- washing your body with
- cleaning your home with

And when you take the time to realize that you are actually the only one responsible for all of your choices, you might make some changes.

The point of ill health is that our bodies are talking to us. Some of listen and run off to a conventional medicine doctor, a.k.a. symptom manager, until that process no longer works.

Others may go to the Internet and find all kinds of conflicting information and throw their hands up in despair.

Others may do so much required research, find a good health practitioner, and work with him or her in order to restore good health.

We often take our health for granted, until something out of the ordinary happens to us, or to a loved one then we are suddenly interested. But good health requires preventive measures, too. Health requires good nutrition. Health requires awareness of what you are putting into your body and on your skin.

Remember your skin is your largest organ and what goes onto it and gets absorbed into it and gets into your blood system.

Unfortunately, we have inferior laws in both Canada and the United States. Most product labels are exceedingly misleading whether in the health food industry or not. Companies don't have you to tell a vast number of things. They can tell you all kinds of false things. Just to give you an idea of what I mean, let's look at a few:

Low fat usually means that there are toxic chemicals or additives, salt and sugar, that have been added to compensate for reduced sweetness.

Labels that claim real fruit may be 90-100% artificial.

So What's the Point?

"Organic" is a widely used and abused term. It is important to know what it means for the products you are purchasing.

Bottled water is no better than tap water and in most cases is even more acidic. Also, according to the Natural Resources Defense Council and the University of Geneva, 25% of bottled water *is* just tap water.

"Multi-grain" is another misleading word suggesting the grains are actually "whole grain" when the product can really be no better for you than those made from refined grains like white flour.

"Natural" theoretically means that the product is made without artificial ingredients, but don't forget that white flour, sugar, and even high-fructose corn syrup are all derived from "natural" ingredients and they are also all highly refined and not at all close to their original form.

When we become unwell, our bodies may be telling us that it needs real nutrients rather than processed toxins. But what happens when you are sick and you go to the physician and he or she puts you on a prescription drug? Ask yourself if the prescription is going to manage the symptoms or eliminate the problem. I suspect that nine chances out of ten it is only going to manage the problem.

Your body isn't asking you to manage the problem; it's asking you fix the underlying cause of the problem.

- Fortunately, you have lots of choices:
- Start eating a whole food diet.
- Start getting good supplements (some research is required here). Many health food store products are not what they claim to be. You may need to talk with someone who knows how to research products:
  - Where were they grown and how healthy the soils are.
  - How were they grown – agriculturally or wild crafted.
  - How were they harvested – time of day, time of season, time of year.
  - How are they processed – how much did man get involved in the processing. Are they using stearates, for example?
  - What was the extraction process?
  - If laboratory – are they mirror images of what our bodies require.
  - Is the bottle accurate, i.e. is Vitamin D3 all D3 or is it actually 60% D2?

So What's the Point?

These are good reasons to connect with a good health practitioner who keeps up with leading edge research, and performs research on the products he or she recommends.

You also have a numerous choices in natural or alternative health practitioners:

- Herbalist
- Nutritionist/Dietician
- Ayurvedic
- TCM/Traditional Chinese Medicine
- Acupuncturist
- Homeopathic

In addition, we know that ultimately we are all made up of energy. So there are also a number of different types of energy healing modalities. While I use several of these methods in my own practice, I do see that if everything is ultimately energy then really any modality of healing is an energy modality.

What I find even stranger is that conventional medicine both utilizes it and negates it. Whether they are using MRIs, CT, or PET scans, x-rays, or other techniques—they are all based on the movement, transformation, and interpretation of energy. Yet, if they cannot charge for the use of equipment then suddenly it has no power? This is one more thing about which you must make your mind.

The following is a list of modalities that are usually considered or referred to as energy modalities:

- Reiki
- Theta
- Qigong
- Reflexology
- Bach Flower remedies
- EMDR – Eye Movement Desensitization and Reprocessing
- OEI – One Eye Integration (a further extension of EMDR)
- EFT – Emotional Freedom Technique
- Meridian Tapping
- TFT - Thought Field Therapy
- Tapas Acupuncture
- Light and Color therapies

So what is the point of all of this? Well, it is very similar to the previous chapter on weight. Your healing journey may be a process of:

- Increasing your awareness of your inner self

- Developing your psychological awareness of what you hold onto, repress, deny, etc.
- Increasing your awareness of your body
- Learning to listen to your body
- Learning to accept your body
- Developing patience, diligence, determination
- Learning what works for your body: type of diet, type of exercise, type of lifestyle

EXERCISE:

1. What kind of healing are you looking for?
   - Physical
   - Emotional
   - Psychological
   - Spiritual

2. Make a list of the growth, learning and awareness you have achieved thus far in your healing journey.

3. Make a list of what you think you might still need to learn.

4. Make a list of what methods of healing have you engaged in.

5. Make a list of what methods of healing you have not explored.

6. Now put together a strategy.

So What's the Point?

CHAPTER 12

Does time contribute to what's the point?

Much of what is presented as "New Age" beliefs is focused around "living in the moment". We explored this back in Chapters 3 and 4. But let's look at this from a different perspective.

With the fast pace of Western societies, the ability to stop and appreciate the moment is lost by many. Westerns are known for getting "stuck" in the past with hurts, disappointments, resentments, etc. or with the "good old days" nostalgia. Others get stuck in the future, always waiting for something to happen that will cure their life ills. For instance:

- When I graduate from high school
- When I get my car
- When I get married
- When I finish university
- When I have children
- When the children leave home
- When I retire…

In this case, life is waiting to happen when something else occurs rather than in the moment. Consequently, life becomes a series of lost moments always waiting for the next event to happen. Thus the introduction of the eastern philosophy to stay in the moment and appreciate the moment became very important.

However, the present doesn't happen without a past and a future in our linear perception of time. Further, given our cognitive strategies and capacities we also need to embrace the past and future, as well as the present.

The following is a simple rule of thumb:

Past————Present————Future

20%—————60%—————20%

If we spend about 20% of our time reviewing the past with the intent to learn, appreciate, and enjoy old memories—then the past becomes an effective component of our lives. Note, the first component was to learn. The past provides a huge opportunity to learn:

- Learn what works
- Learn what doesn't work
- Learn about people – how individuals function, think, feel, make choices

So What's the Point?

- Learn about setting effective boundaries
- Learn about the difference between holding on and letting go
- Learning about the difference between being determined and saying enough is enough
- Learn about when to use humor to soften a situation and when not to
- Learn about the difference between forgiveness and acceptance
- Learn about effective ways to express anger and frustration

Many of these lessons come from challenges we experienced in the past. If we take a moment to review and reflect on past experiences and actually do the learning, we gain wisdom. If we don't do the learning, life is usually patient enough to provide the lessons to us over and over again until we learn the lessons we need to learn.

Now, the future is equally important because we need to identify where we want to go and how we plan to get there. If we don't decide where we want to go and how to get there, we often end up going around in circles, only realizing years later that we are in the same spot where we started out.

If we are wise enough to set goals and determine a pathway to get there, we can come up with two possible options:

- We may get caught up in our perception of what we have to achieve and lose out on various other opportunities OR waste time on a path we are not meant to be.

- We may be wise enough to set the goals, determine the path, and then allow life to take us where we are meant to go.

Example:

I often provide a personal example of this process from when I first entered university. I went with a vague intent to study and then teach math and physics. I actually wanted to become an astrophysicist but didn't believe I had the smarts to do so.

I set out after my goal, set out the plan then life kept happening and getting in the way. I developed friendships with two women who were very much into psychology. They kept taking all the psychology courses offered and encouraged me to sit in with them. I loved the courses and the exploration of the human mind and brain. There was one professor, in particular, who was a hoot and really knew how to bring a class alive.

So What's the Point?

Both of these women wanted to be psychologists. I had no intention of becoming a psychologist because I couldn't imagine someone actually needing a psychologist to help them get through life. However, I was fascinated by the theories that said that both the brain and the mind were one and the same, or that they were two different processes.

I was also fascinated to learn how different "normal" could be, (never mind all the abnormalities). Well, these two student friends of mine applied for the BA Honors program, so I did, too. My thesis actually had positive results. When they applied to graduate school, I did, too. And I was the only one of the three of us who got in. Imagine that! I went into university to become a teacher of math and physics but came out a psychologist.

The moral of the story is, set your goals, determine your strategy, and take advantage of all that life offers you. Often, you will end up in an entirely different place than where you anticipated but you will end up ahead of where you started rather than going around in circles.

Obviously, it may not happen like this for everyone. You may end up where you had intended and you may find:

- That you absolutely hate it and that it was not what you had anticipated.

- You absolutely love it and it was and still is your passion.

If you find that it is not what you thought it would be then there are a couple of lessons that you may need to learn:

- Did you miss signposts along the way that might lead you down a different path?
- Are you meant to be here so that you can recognize that you romanticize places, positions, and relationships in your life and you need to learn to have a better compass?
- Do you need to learn when to say, "Enough is enough" and move on?
- Do you need to learn to embrace change?

The following is a list of questions you may ask yourself. Some of them may appear contradictory on the surface but truly living means embracing the full spectrum and not limiting yourself.

Time, is it working for you or against you?

Are you going too fast to recognize when the road made a detour?

- Are you stuck in the past?
- Are you waiting for the future to happen before you start living your life?

- Are you able to easily shift from the past to the present, from the future to the present?
- Are you able to stay focused in the present?
- Do you live your life with intent or simply allow it to happen to you?
- Do you fret that life is moving too fast?
- Do you live each day to the fullest?
- Do you take time to really appreciate the moment?

EXERCISE:

1. Identify what time means for you.
2. If you knew that you were going to die tomorrow, what would you do with your time today?
3. If you knew that you had thirty years left to live, what would you do with your time today? In the next year? In the next five years?
4. Do you feel stuck in life or do you feel that you are moving effectively through your life?
    - If you feel stuck – what could you do differently today, tomorrow, or next week, to start creating a different pattern?
    - Do you make excuses for staying stuck?

- Do you rationalize and justify staying stuck, i.e. are you hiding behind responsibilities, people, jobs, etc.?

So What's the Point?

CHAPTER 13

What purpose does this question serve in our lives?

What is the point? Does the question have a purpose? I believe it does.

It pushes us to go beyond our current belief structure. It encourages us to reach further spiritually, intellectually, emotionally, physically, sexually, and socially. As human beings we appear to have an innate drive to go further, but many of us lose that drive as we grow older.

One might suggest that the primary purpose of other species would appear to be a combination of: to propagate, to adapt to one's environment, and to stay in ecological balance so as to maintain the full ecological balance. Human beings, on the other hand, appear to have a somewhat different agenda. In a relatively short period of time, we have grown and learned a great deal both negatively and positively. Unfortunately, this has occurred at a great cost to both the earth itself and to both our own and other species.

From an evolutionary perspective, this different agenda is presumably, at least in part, a reflection of the development of the frontal lobe and cerebral cortex of the brain.

Christianity would have us believe that this is because God gave us a spirit, something the other species or nature don't have.

Aboriginal cultures around the world claim that plants and animals also have souls.

Buddhism would have us believe that God is not separate from the universe and as such, a creator thereof, but rather is in and of everything and as such is "more than the sum of the parts".

Regardless of the belief system, there certainly appears to be something different about humans. From the perspective of this book, we are the only species that questions who we are and looks for purpose in our being. (At least as far as we know.)

While we can assume that we are the only species that seems to push ourselves further intellectually, and subsequently in other arenas of our lives, the recognition of that ability does not answer what the purpose of the ability is. So let's go back to the questions.

The first question is: what is the point?

And the second question is: what is the purpose in asking such a question?

We could argue that there is neither a point nor a purpose; it is simply a byproduct of an evolutionary development.

The problem with answering such questions in this manner is that it not only leaves us empty but is also a contradiction to the extent that every evolutionary development has occurred either for a reason, or in response to something. So, the ability to ask, "what is the point" must serve a purpose.

If we look for the answers within the context of Christianity (and all other derivatives of the Judaic religion), the church may tell us to leave it with God. Yet, how many Christian philosophers, saints and followers have asked the question? Old Christianity told us not to question God or the Bible, as that was indicative of doubting God, and therefore a sin. Modern Christianity suggests that God gave us a brain and we are meant to use it wisely.

Perhaps to ask, to question, to seek and explore, are ways of honoring God. Thus to answer what is the purpose of the question, one would presumably have to answer, that it is to find, recognize, and honor God.

Buddhist philosophy (and all Buddhist-based philosophies) suggests that we are to go within and contemplate both our separateness from and connectedness to the universe in order to become enlightened. In the process of journeying from one end of this continuum to the other, we would recognize that to the extent that we are all interconnected we should have compassion for one another, no matter how separate we may be in our beliefs, attitudes, and behaviors. The purpose of the question, what is the point, would then be to motivate us to begin on the path of enlightenment, because without it there would be no point.

While there are many religions around the world, there appear to be two primary concepts of God. God is either the creator of the universe and thus separate from it, or in and of the universe and thus a part of it. Either way, the purpose of the question is to motivate us to a more spiritual pathway.

What about those who believe "ashes to ashes and dust to dust"? This might actually have the simplest of answers. If there were no karma or reincarnation or heaven or hell, what would be the purpose in asking, so what's the point?

I propose that the purpose is to drive us to simply maximize who we are. Granted, this does not always appear to work out well. For instance, when some ask the question and in their despair they cannot find a suitable answer, they commit suicide.

One might say that they committed the ultimate sin or crime. Another might have compassion and say that they could not find the resources they needed to carry on. One might say, well if they could not find a purpose to their lives then perhaps they should end it. While a seemingly cold answer, perhaps the belief that suicide is a horrible crime or sin is really the cold way of operating. There have been many societies throughout history that honored death and dying very differently. Further, we are more kind to animals than we are to humans when it comes to death and dying. For instance, when an animal is suffering and we cannot help him, we will honor and respect him by putting him down, as opposed to keeping him alive and suffering so that we do not have to grieve its loss.

The flip side of the coin is that for those who have no belief in an afterlife (although we can track our morphic energetic fields, after death, we have no idea of what this means on a scientific level, but we still abound with beliefs), it may allow some of these people to indulge in greed and selfishness without any contrition. Some may come up empty inside, and when they confront the emptiness they usually ask, so what's the point?

EXERCISE:

1. Identify what your beliefs are about this life, i.e. how and why are we here?

2. Identify what your beliefs are about the afterlife, i.e. what happens to our energy, our soul, our beliefs, when the physical body dies?

3. Explore whether or not you are living your life in alignment with your beliefs.

CHAPTER 14

Conclusion

So what's the point? What was the point of this book?

We have explored from the most horrific to the easy and workable. Why? To provoke people to explore whom they are outside of the confines, limitations, and beliefs they had already created.

For those who stuck it out and continued to ask the question, it might push them to go beyond the scientific justification and rationalizations that they have learned to depend on.

For some, it might create a different perspective in their lives that allows them to move forward with gratitude and appreciation.

For others, it may provoke a deeper look at who they are on a number of different levels of life—emotionally, psychologically, intellectually, and spiritually.

For others, they might explore who they are on a more materialistic level—physically, sexually, socially, and financially.

For others, it may provoke an awareness of how many choices we have in life:

- We can choose to make goals.
- We can choose a strategy to achieve the goal.
- We can choose to take advantage of opportunities along the way.
- We can choose to expand our awareness of:
  - Who we are as human beings
  - Who we are physically
  - Who we are emotionally
  - Who we are psychologically
  - Who we are spiritually
  - Who we are in business
- We can choose to embrace the path we are on.
- We can choose to alter our path.
- We can choose to alter our beliefs and attitudes.
- We can choose to operate with more acceptance and compassion for others.
- We can choose to persist with determination and creativity.
- We can choose to say "enough is enough" and walk away.

So What's the Point?

- We can choose to stay stuck where we are or choose to move.
- We can choose to change the way we operate or not.
- We can choose to find ways that allow us to gain our optimal potential.

So what's the point?

- To develop a greater awareness of who we are.
- To make conscious choices.
- To take responsibility for our choices, with conscious intent.
- To accept who we currently are while embracing the choices that allow us to reach our greatest potential.

So perhaps, the point of asking, "What is the point?" is to help us be aware of our choices, rather than simply existing, thus providing us with the choice to live our lives to our fullest potential.

Enjoy your journey with the choices you have. I hope you choose never to stay stuck. I hope you choose to live life to its fullest on every level.

www.ingramcontent.com/pod-product-compliance
Lightning Source LLC
Chambersburg PA
CBHW072009090426
42734CB00033B/2212